30 CELTIC KNOTS
AND
KALEIDOSCOPES
TO COLOR

VARIATIONS ON A THEME

LYRIC MONTGOMERY KINARD

www.LyricKinard.com

Helpful Hints

I love to slice out pages with an X-Acto knife and color them one at a time.

Try using a clipboard on your lap, held at an angle to reduce neck strain.

(Am I the only one who holds my head an an angle and bites my tongue while I color?)

Pencils

When using pencils, color in shapes lightly on your first pass.

On your second pass press harder to darken just the inside edges of a shape.

Try blending colors, especially lighter ones in the center of a shape.

Markers

Each design is printed on only one side of the page to prevent bleed-though.

When coloring in the book, place a blank paper behind your design as a blotter.

Add shades with a color just one step over on the color wheel.

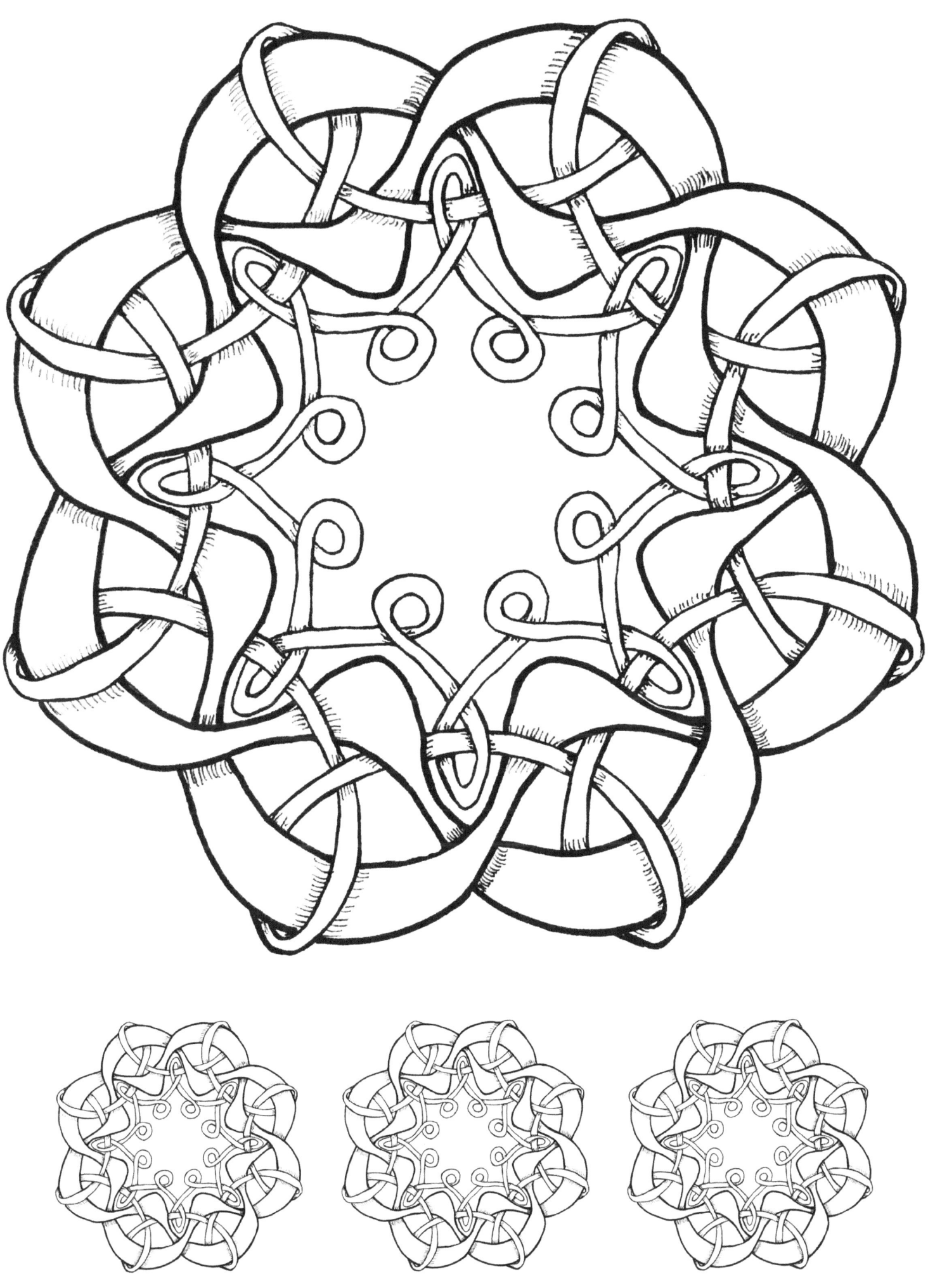

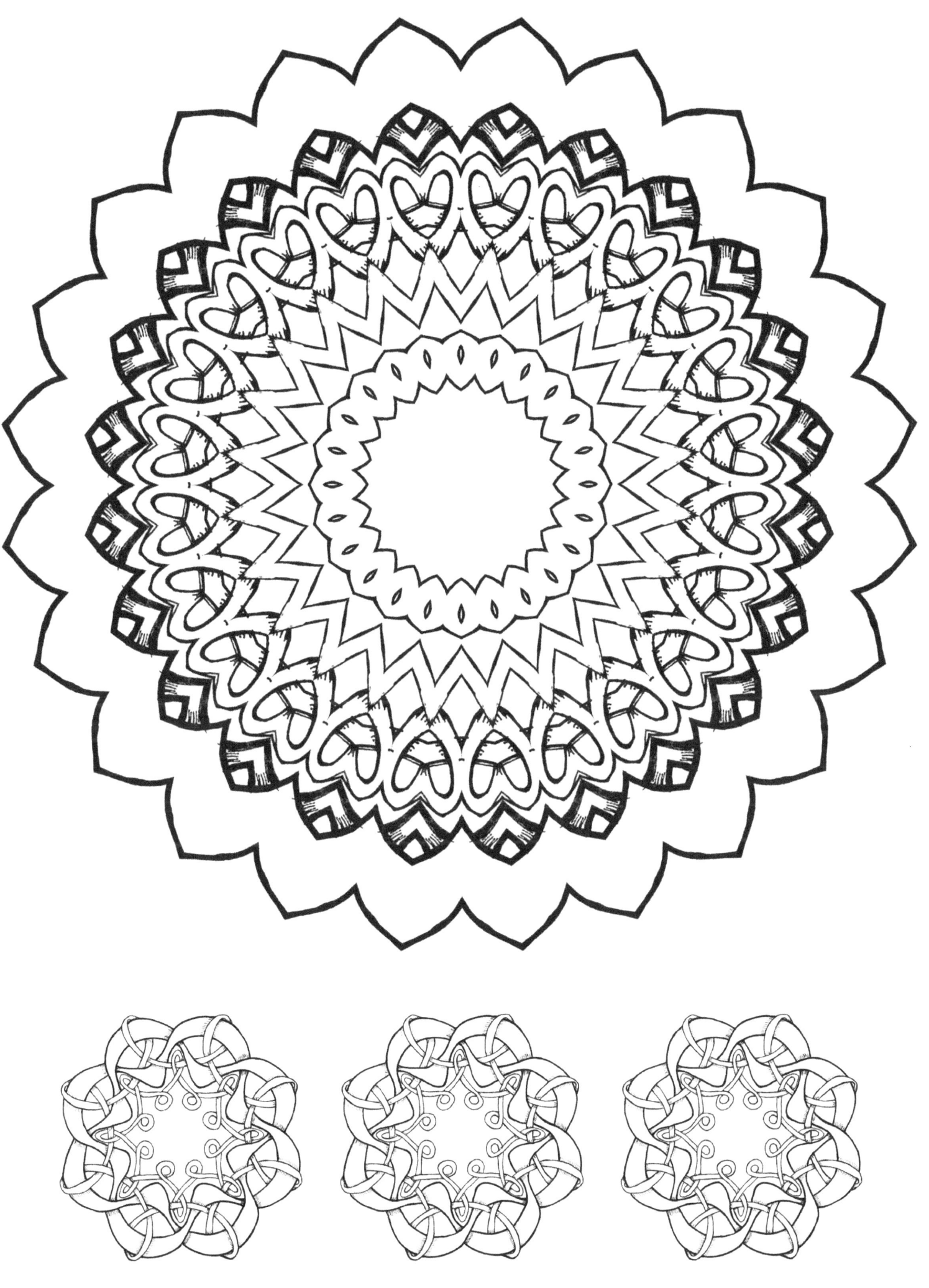

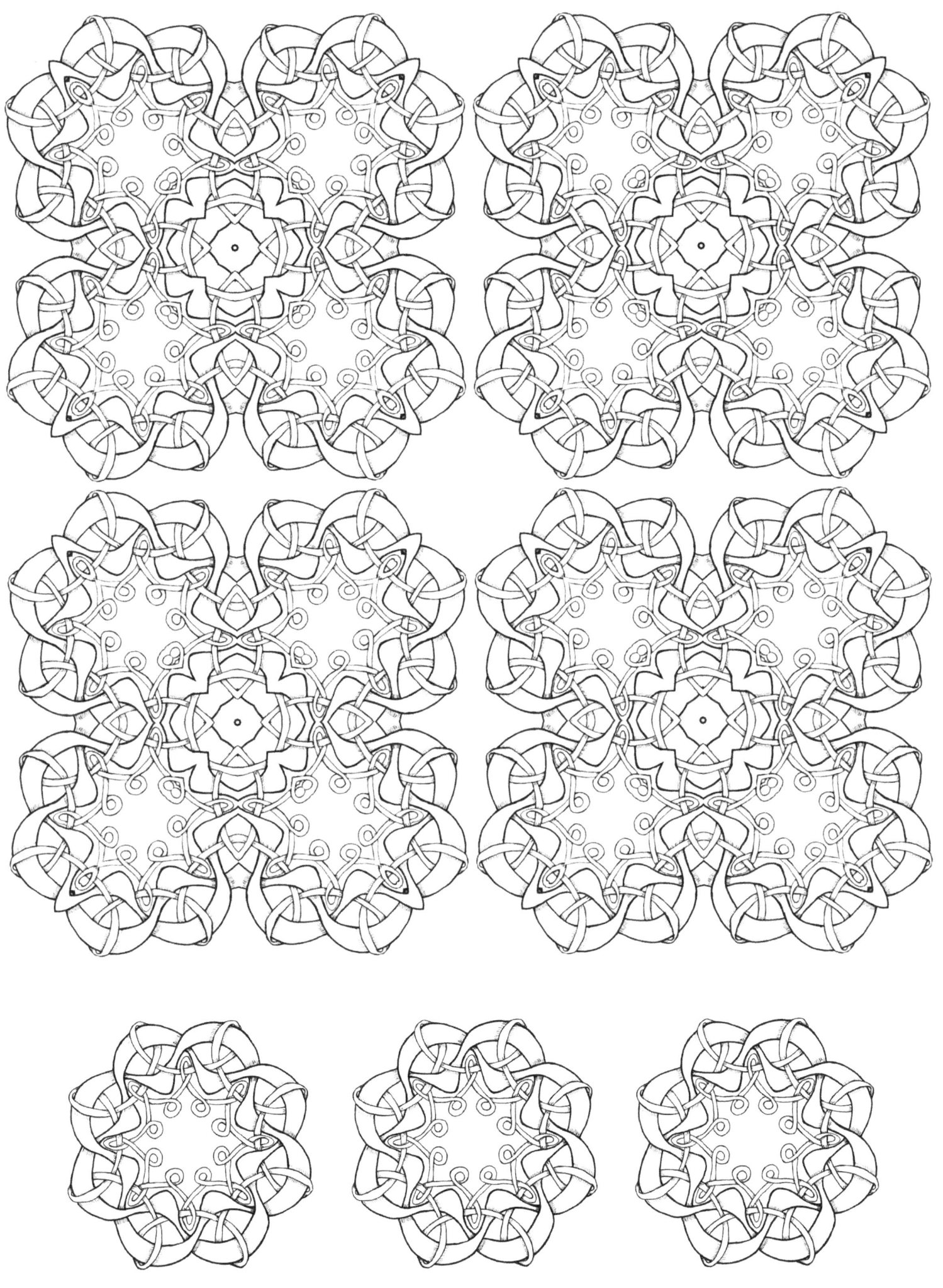

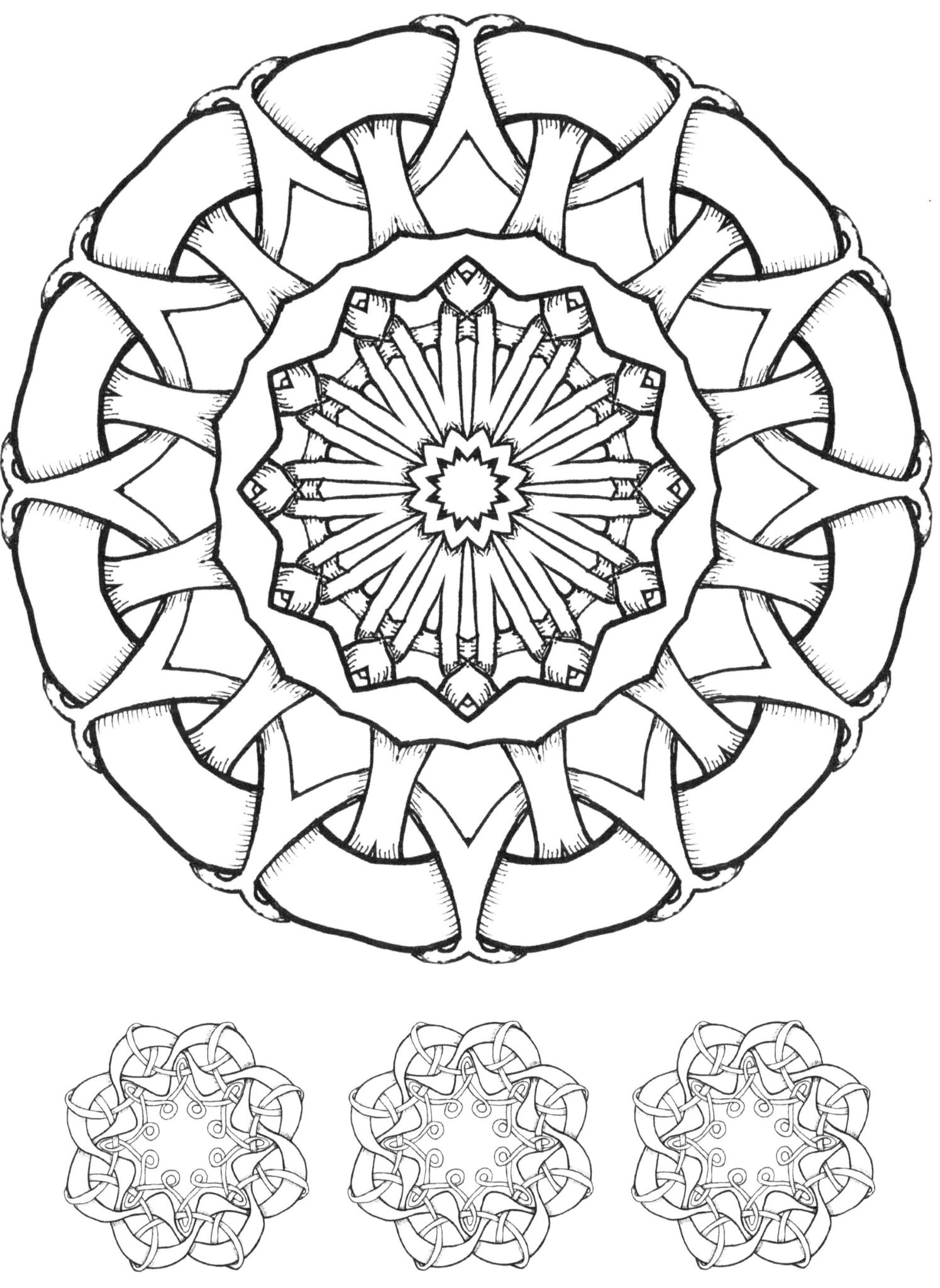

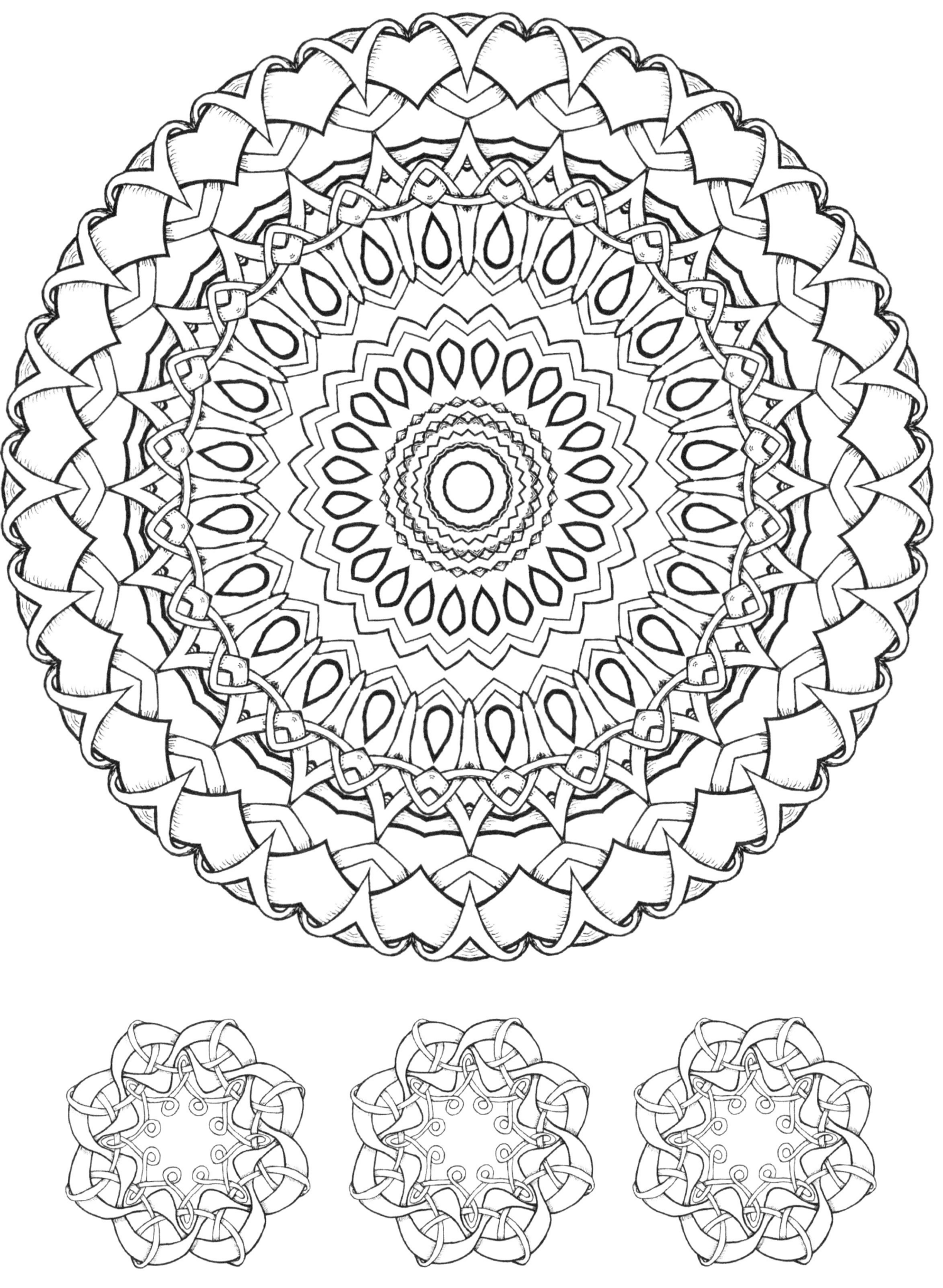

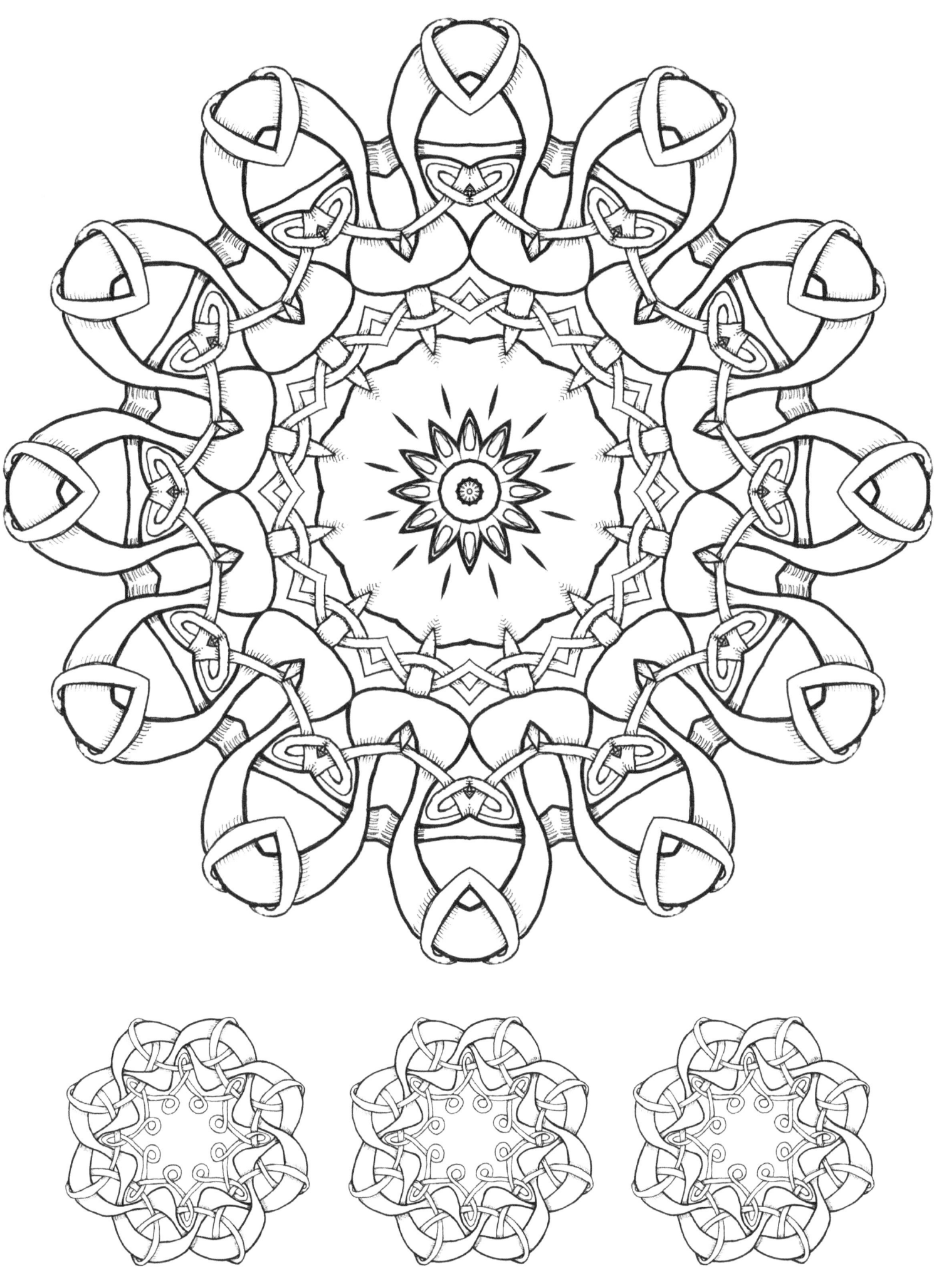

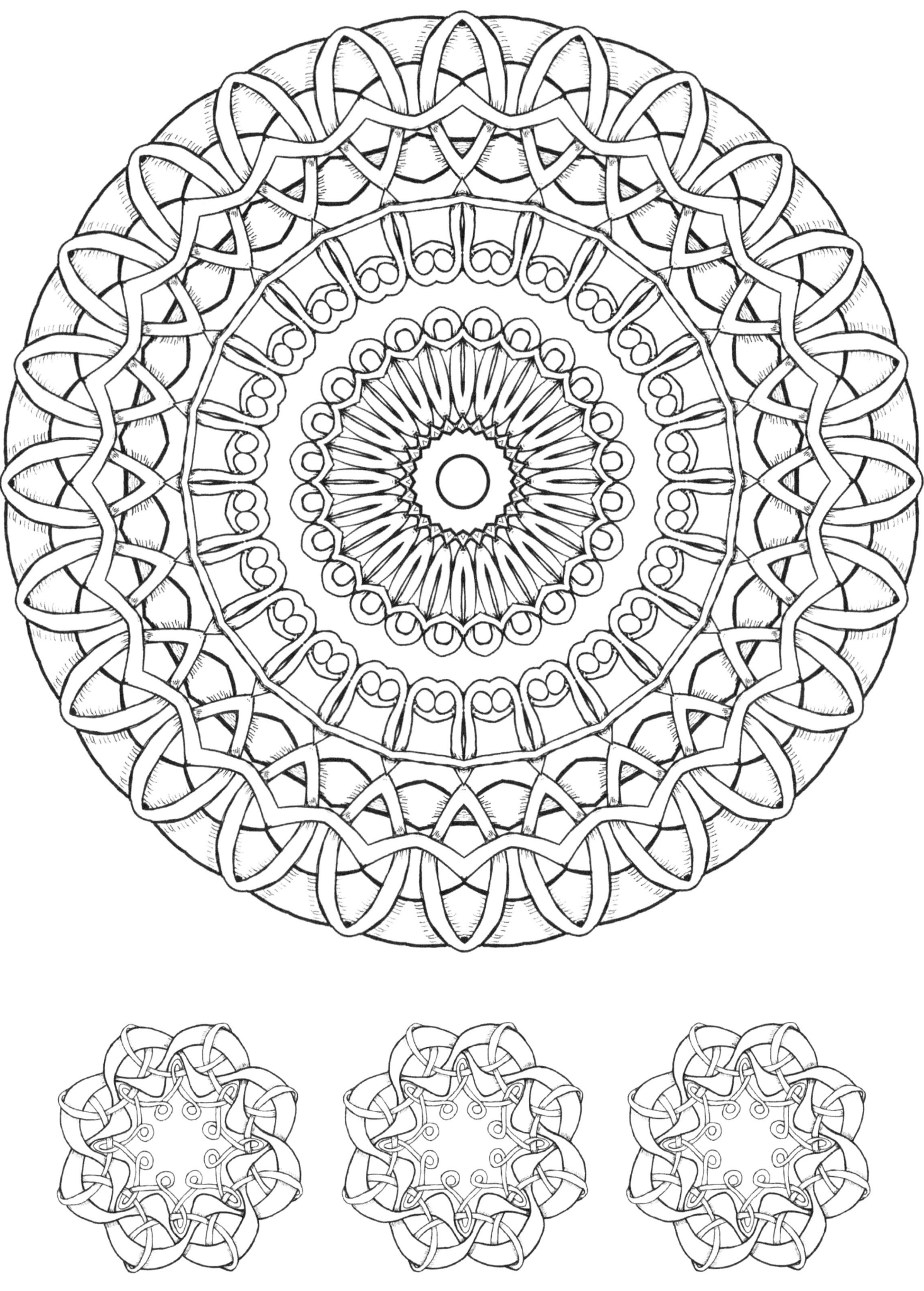

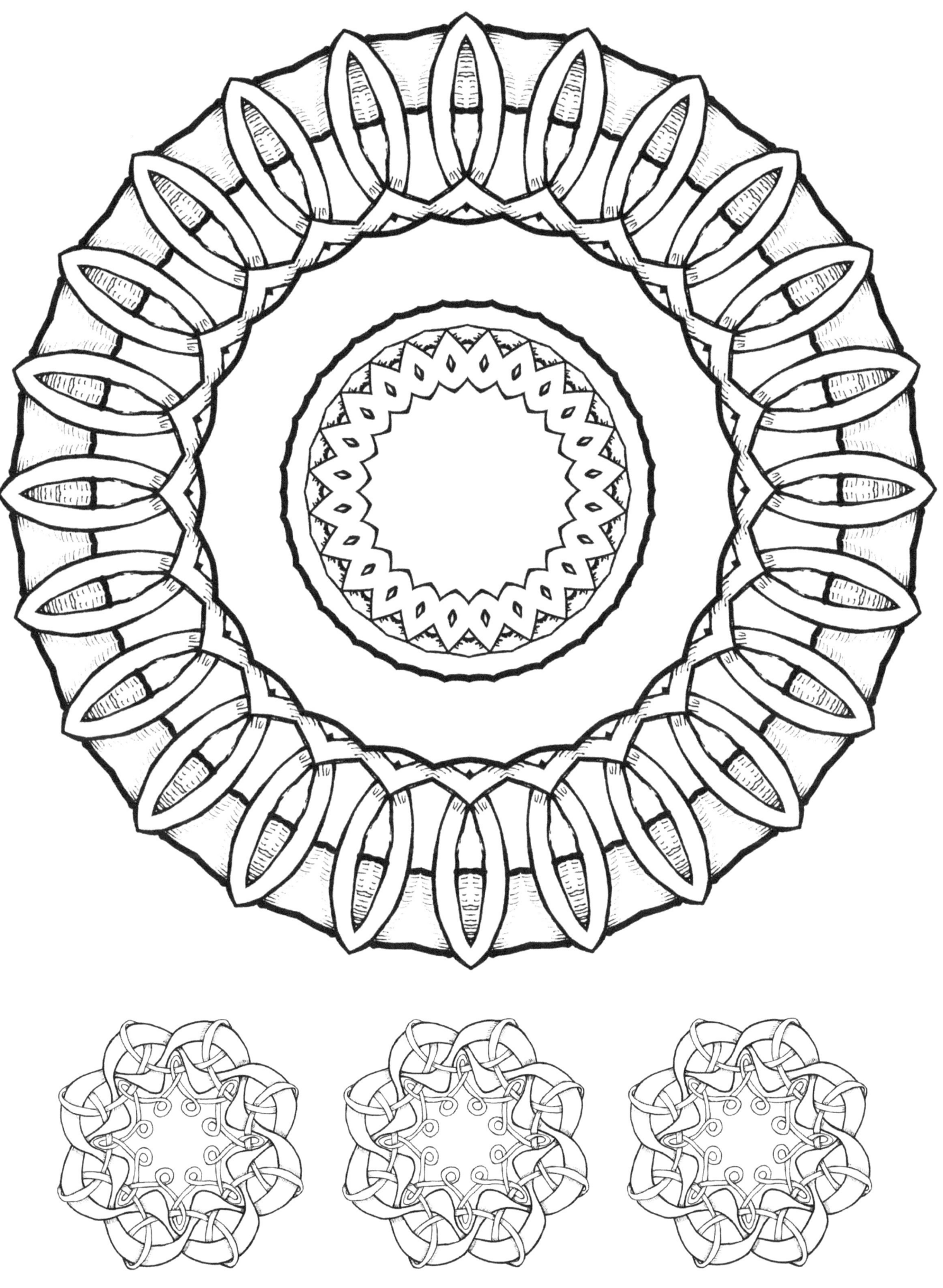

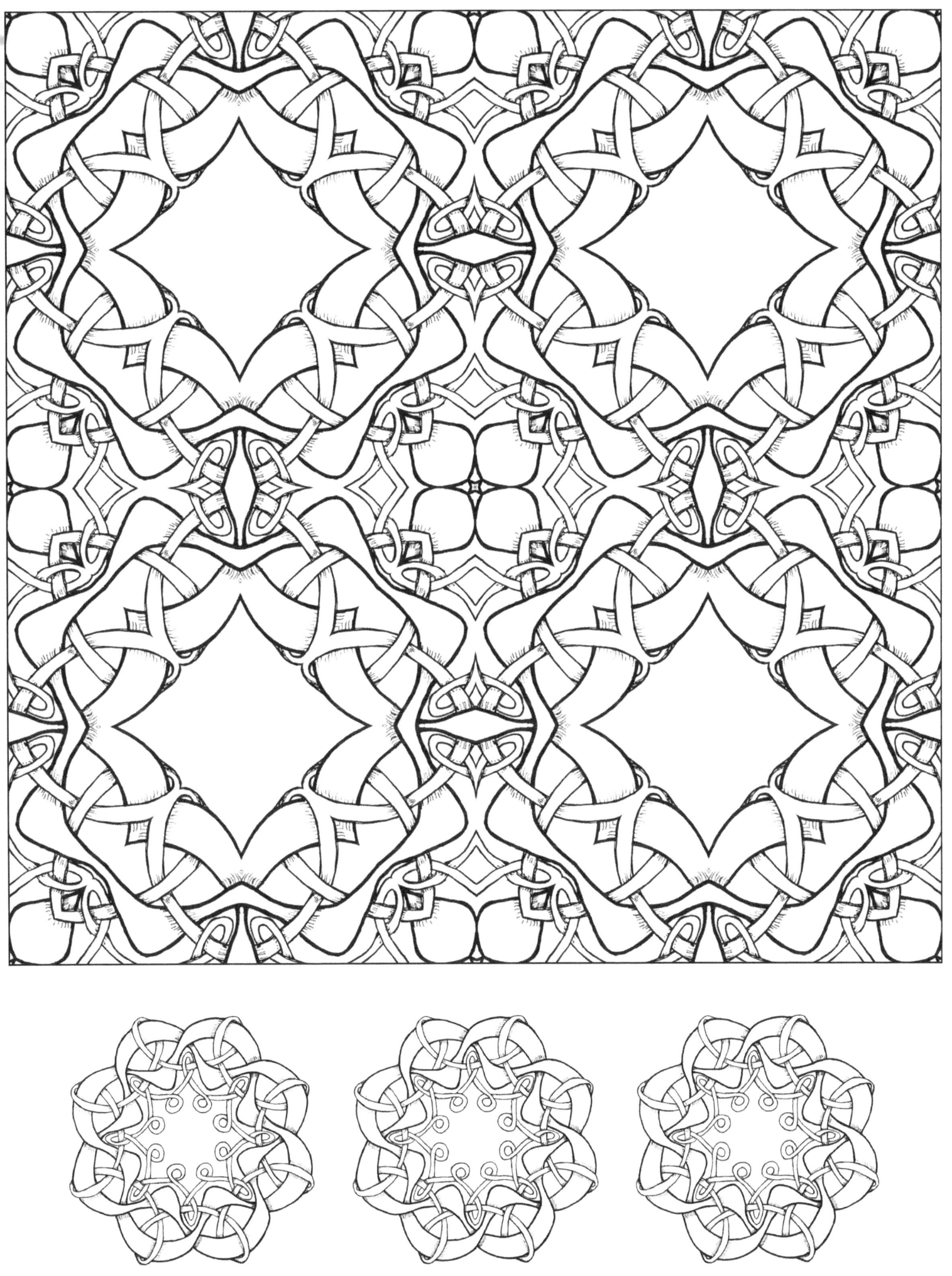

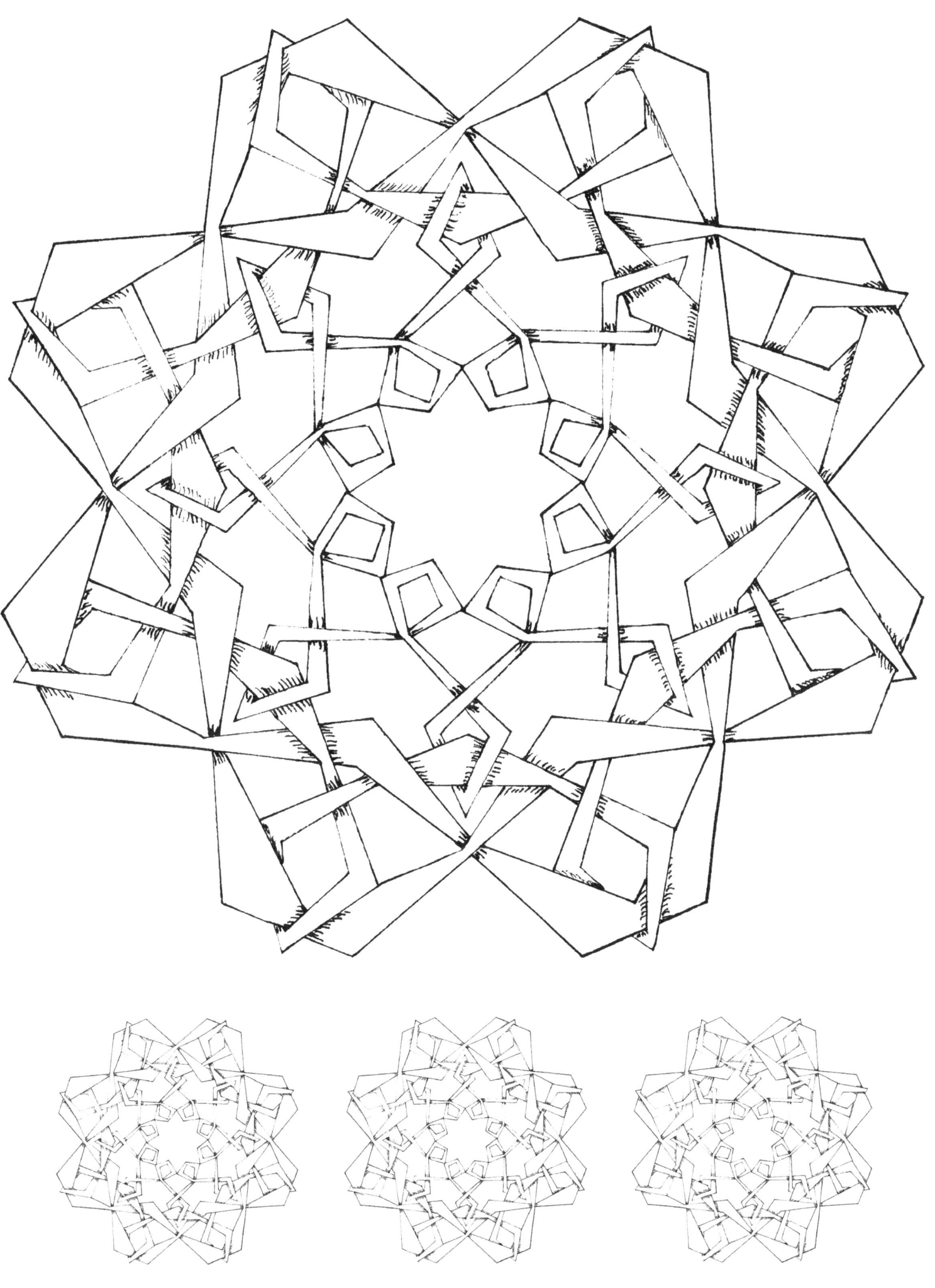

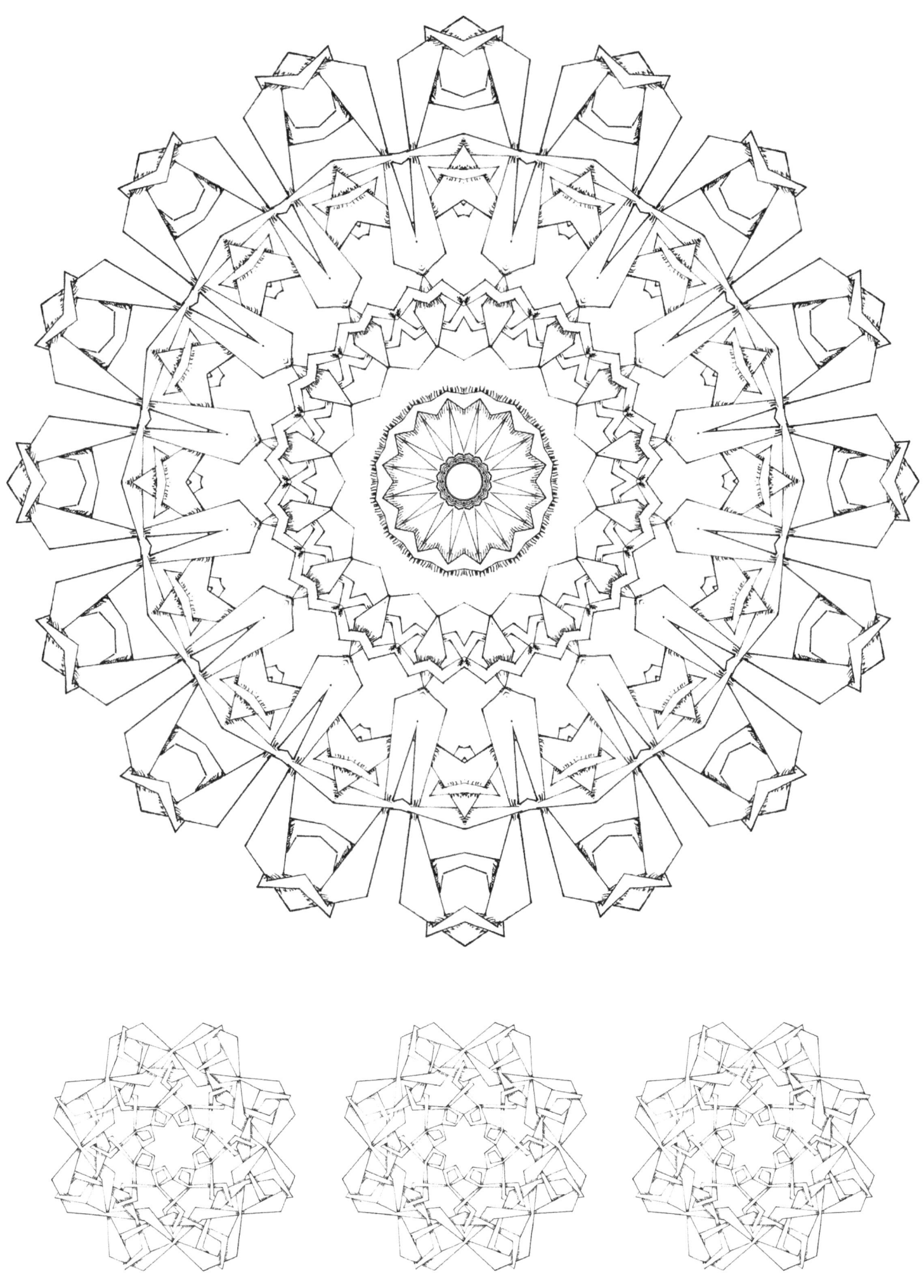

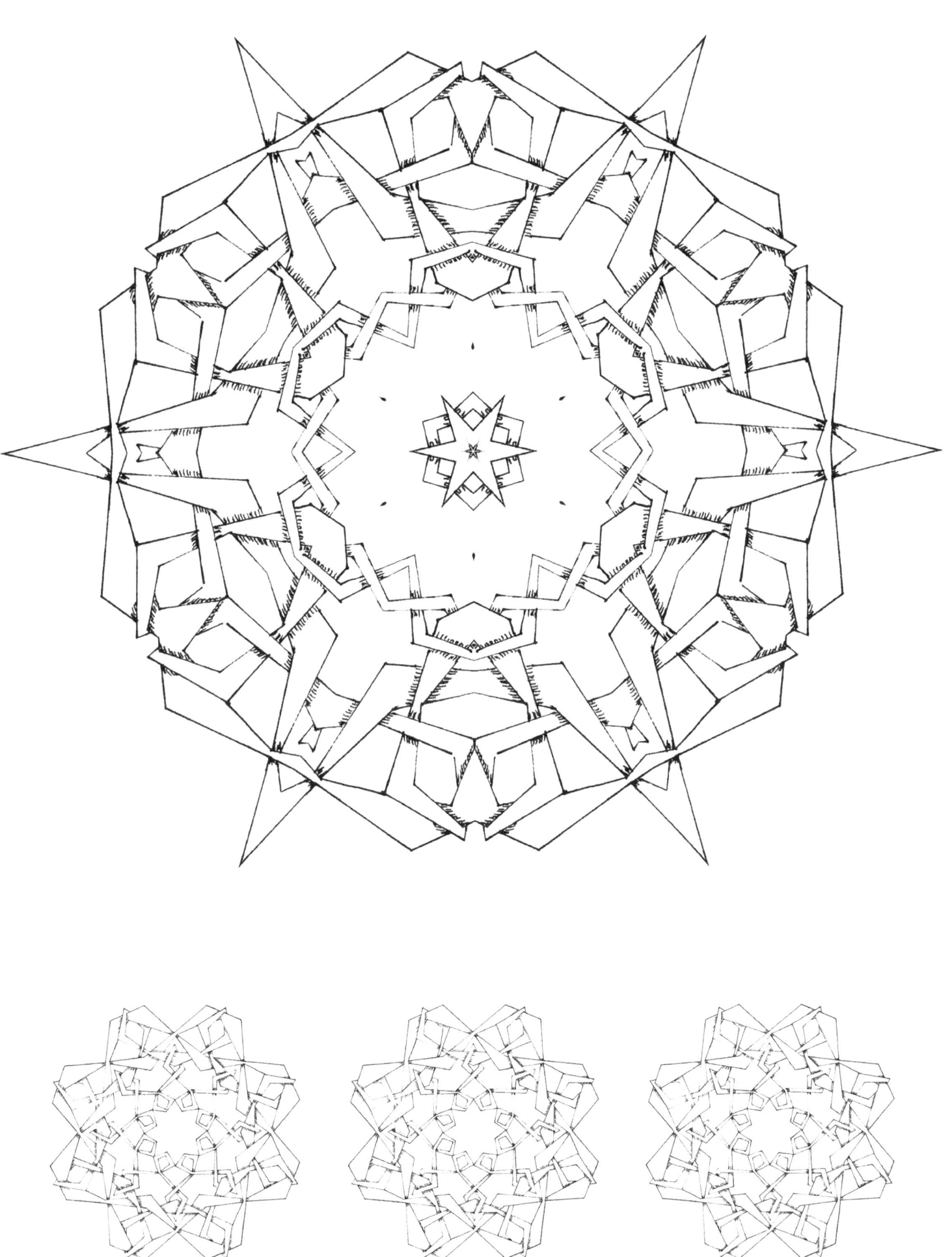

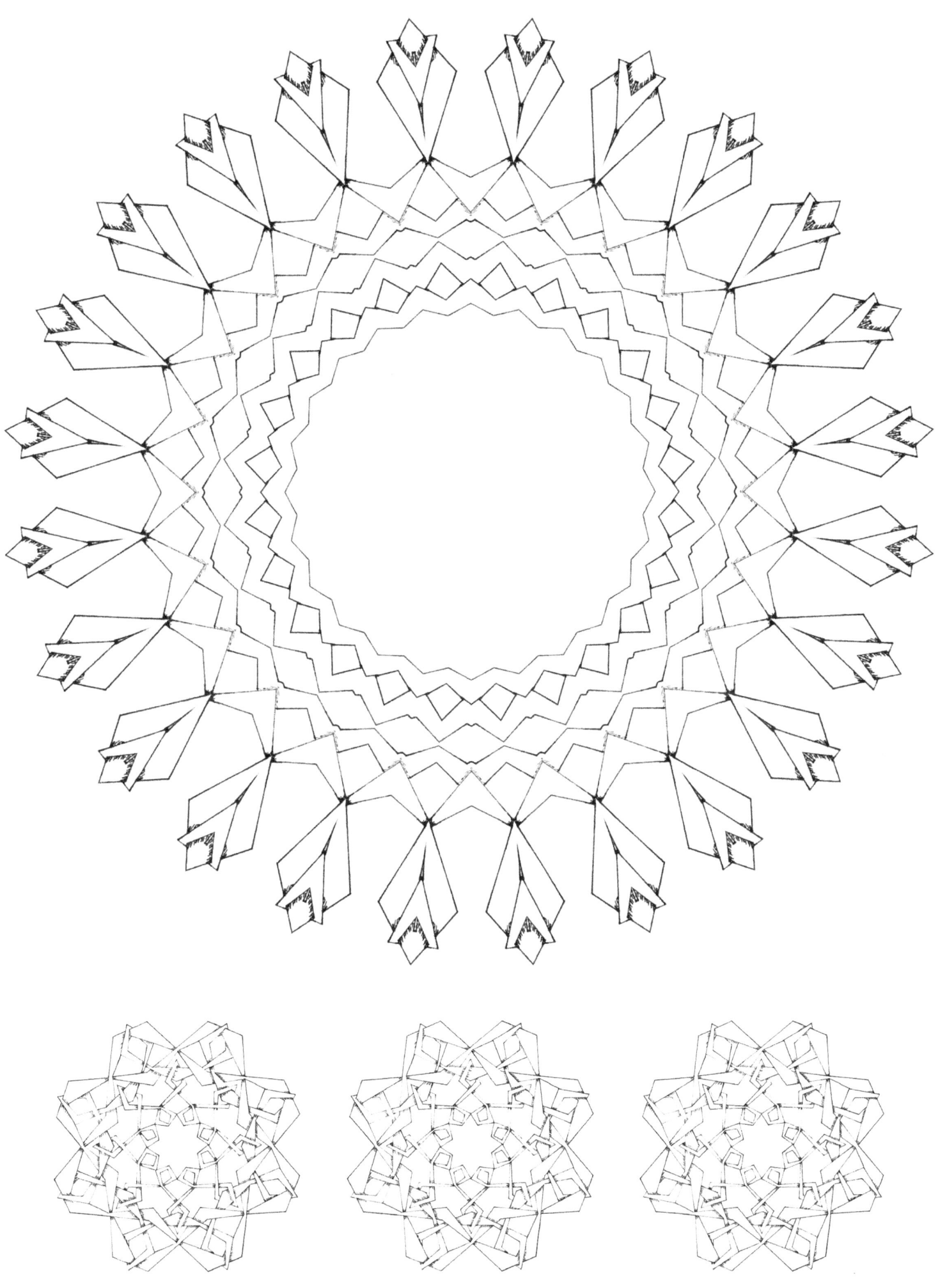

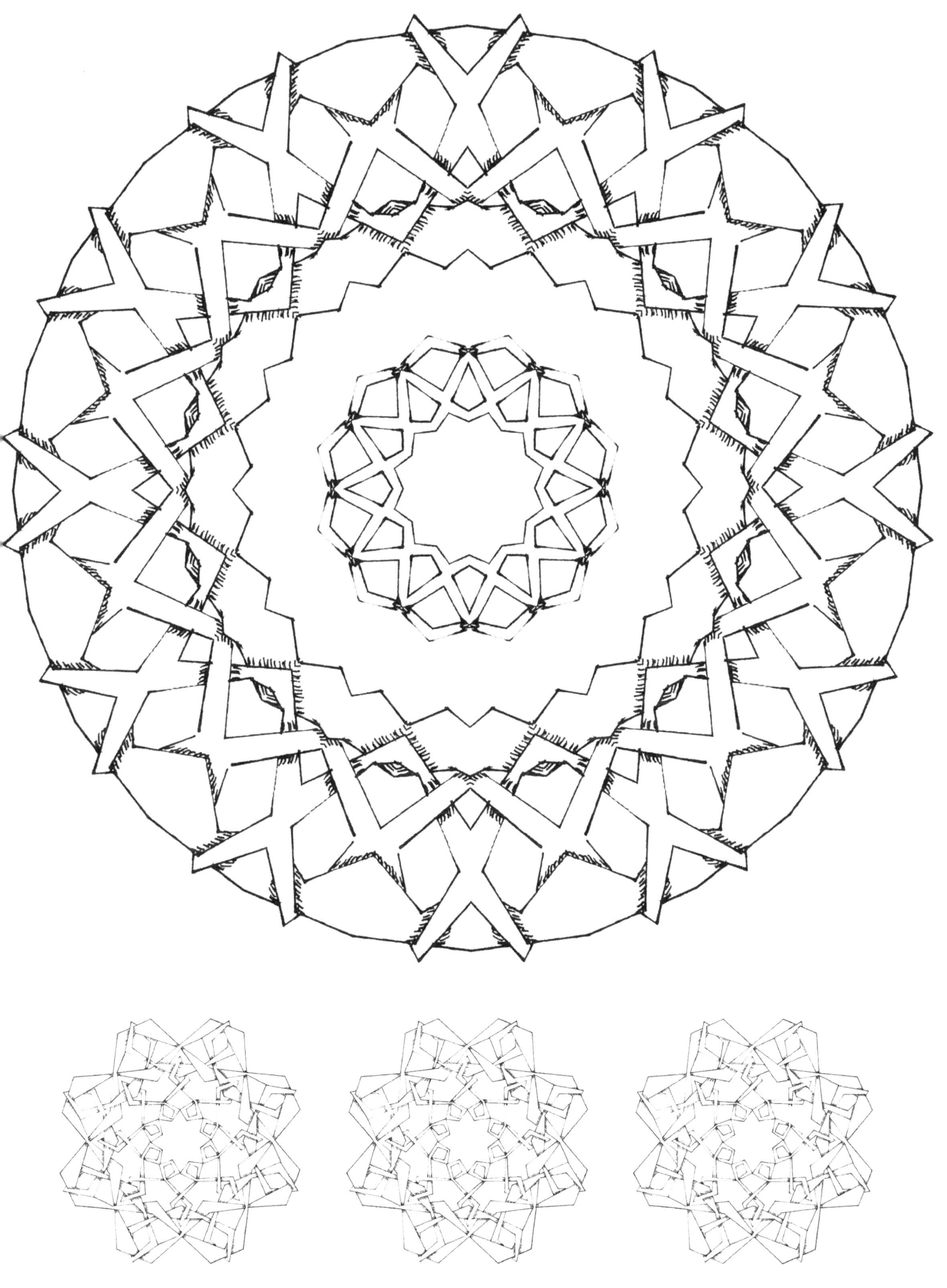

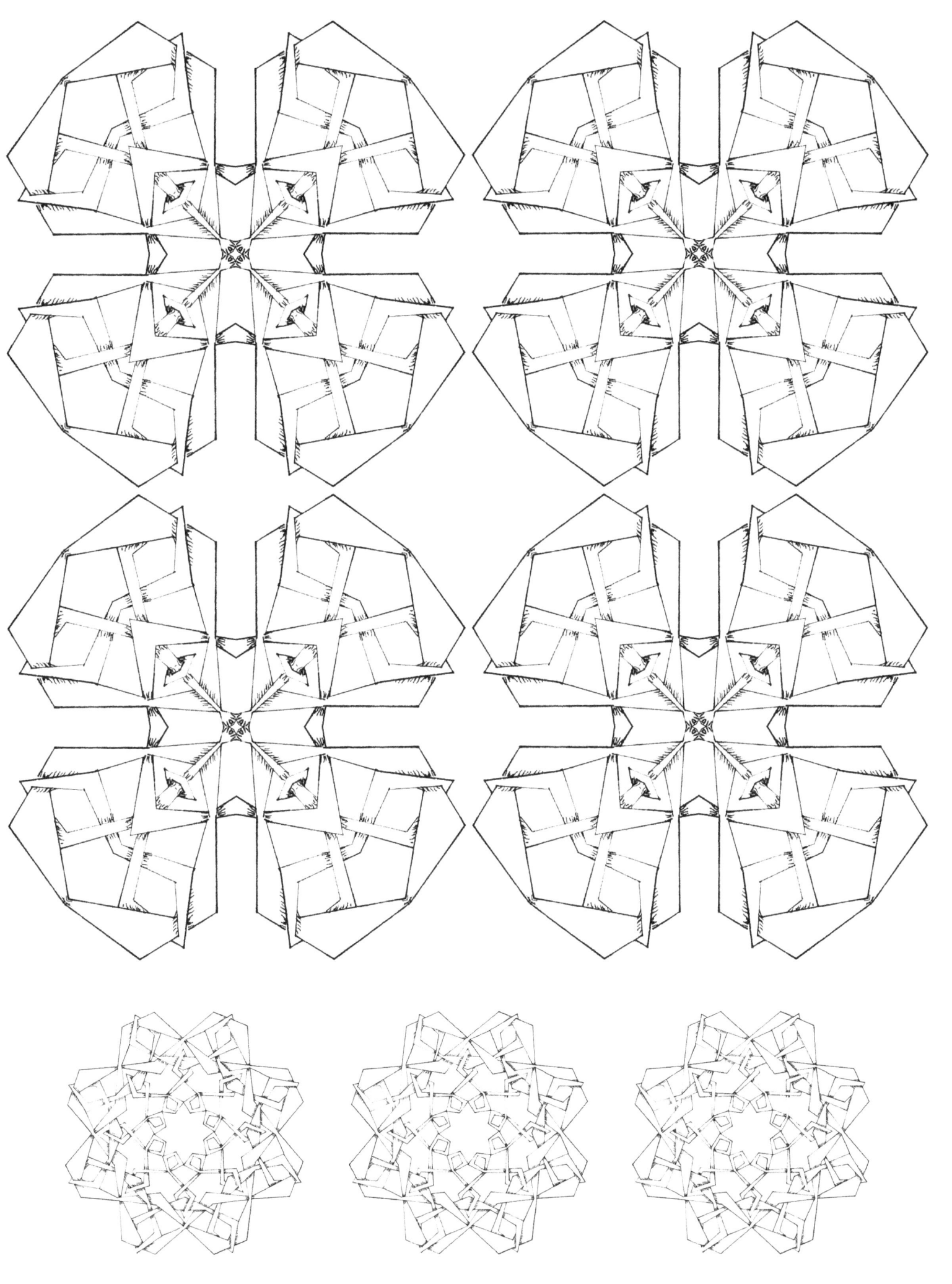

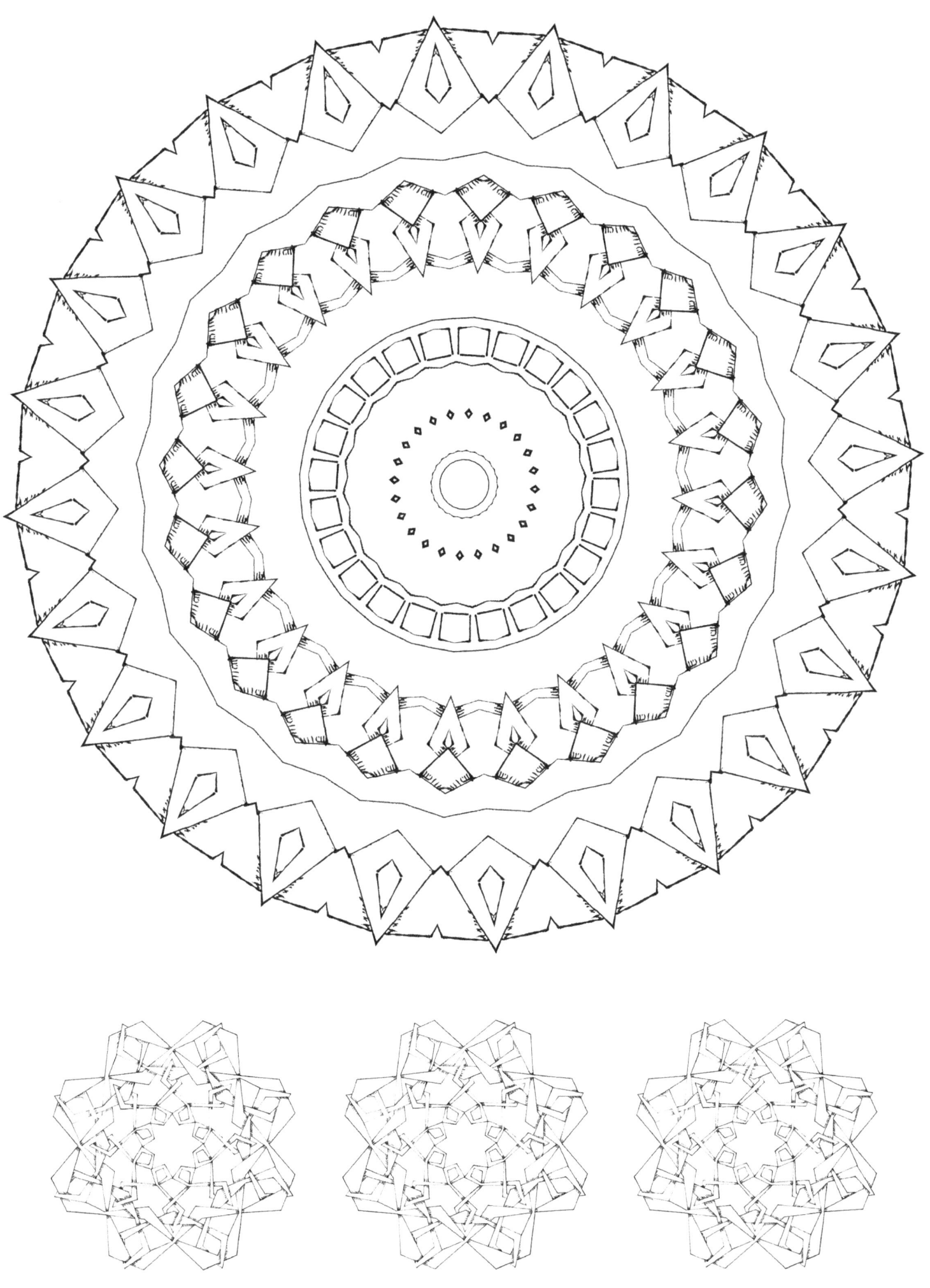

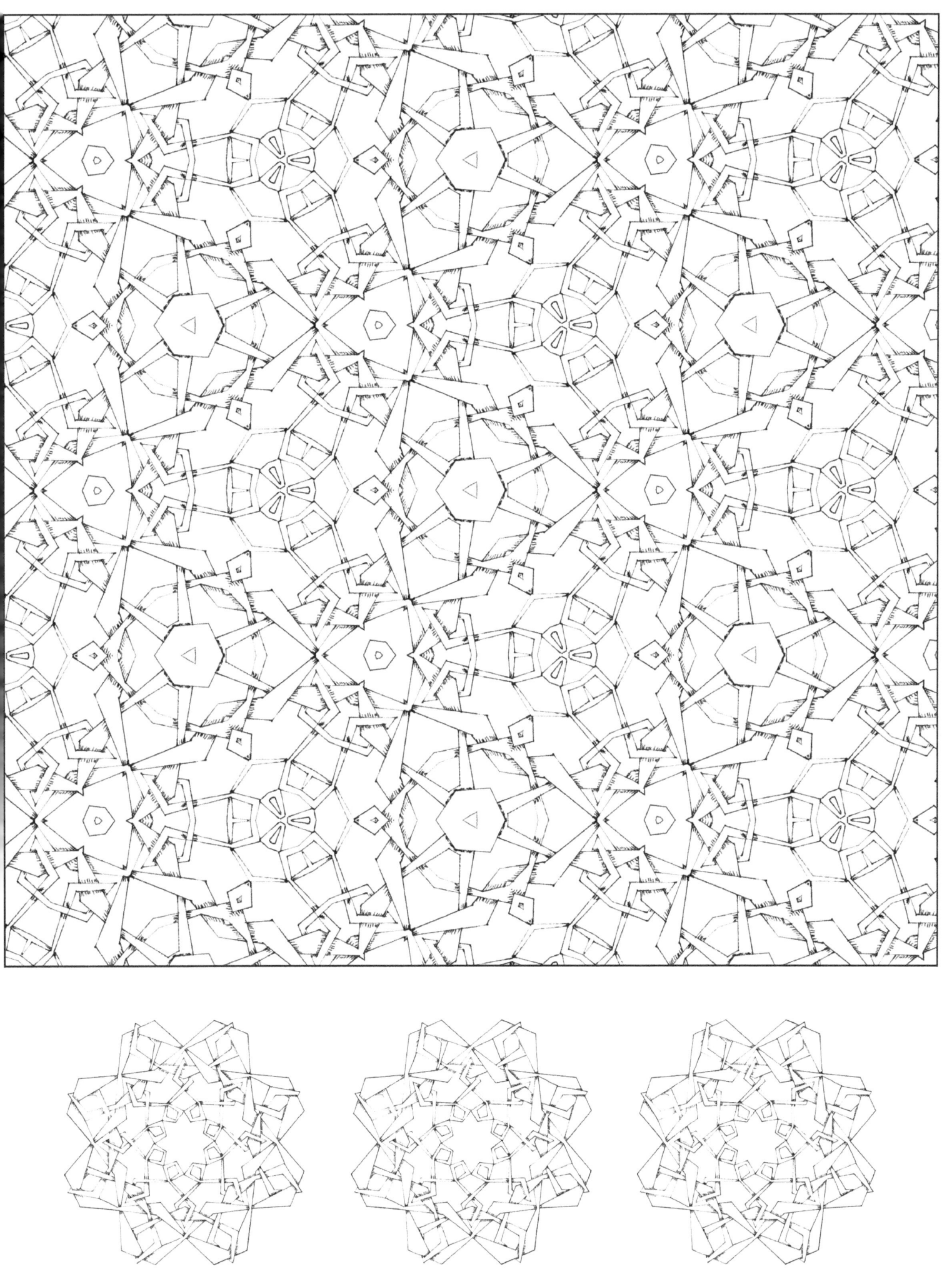

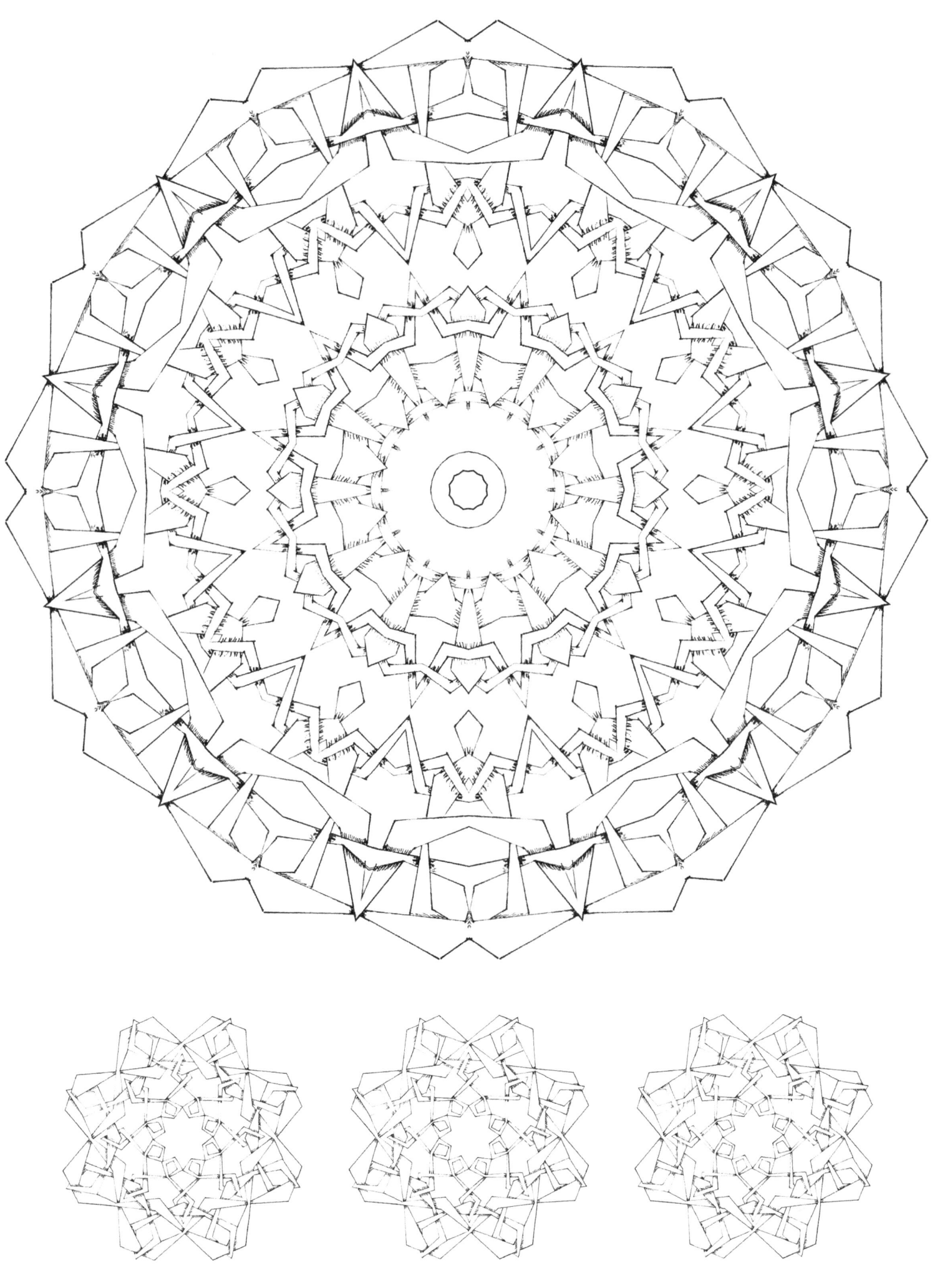

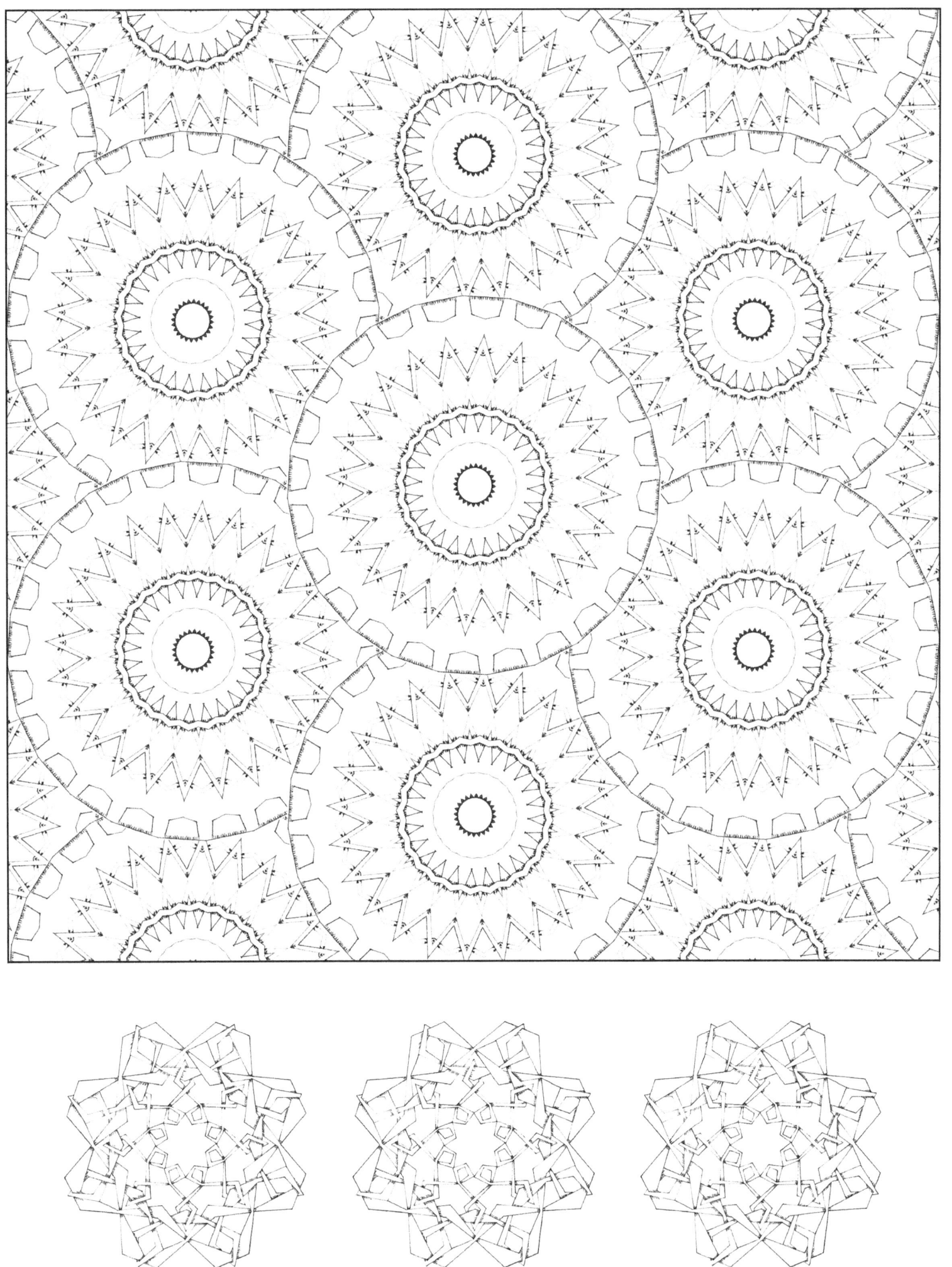

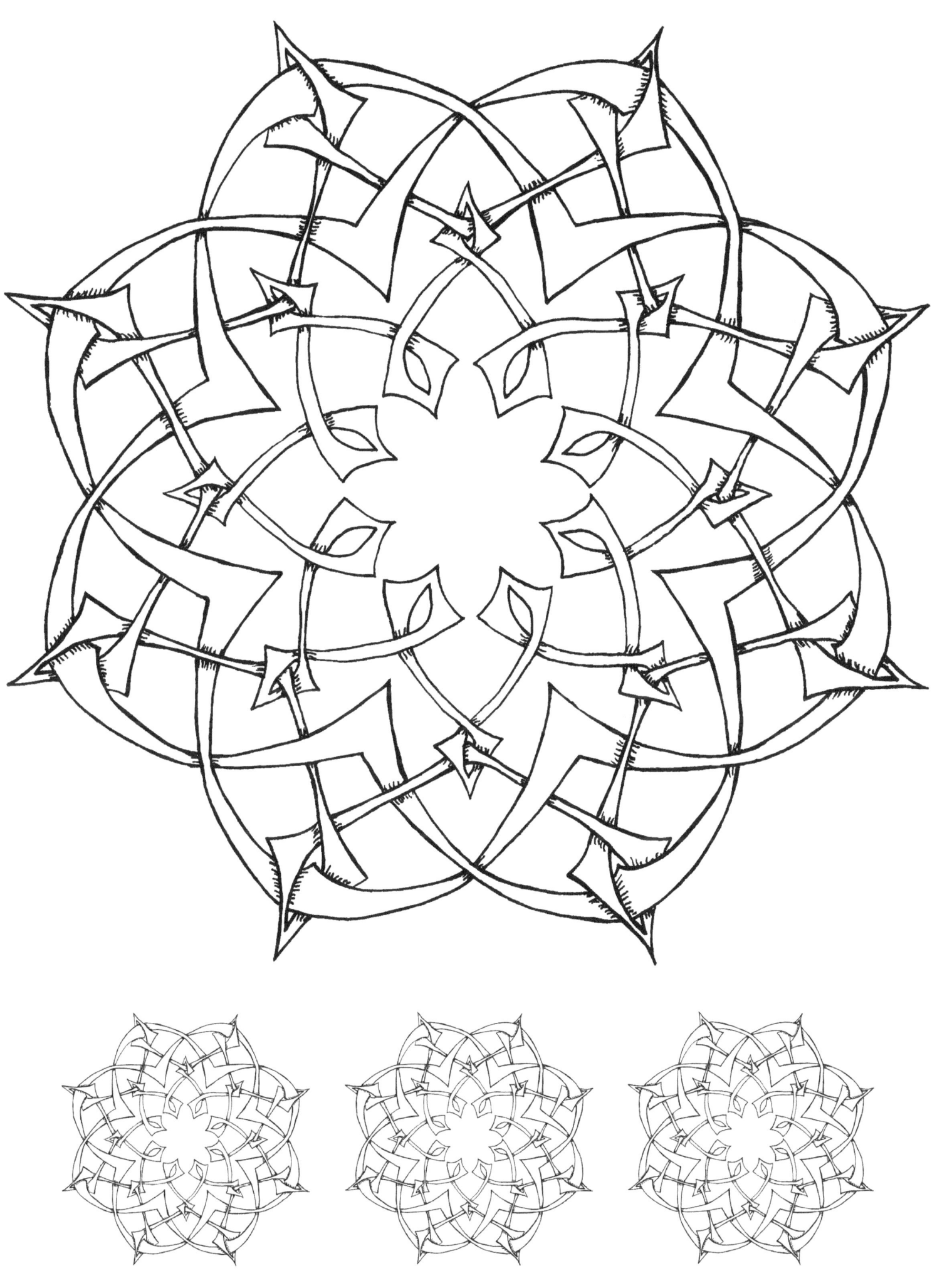

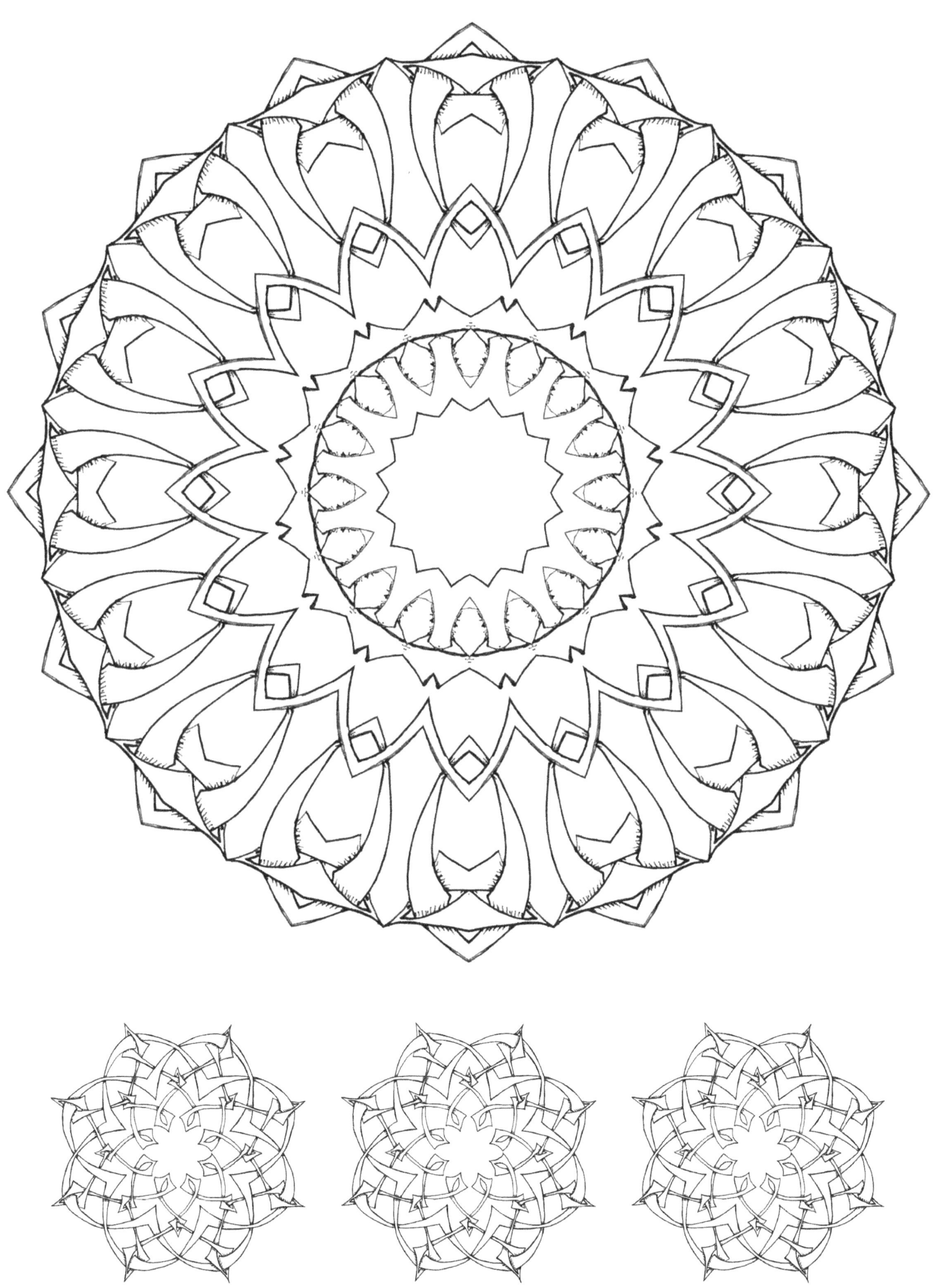

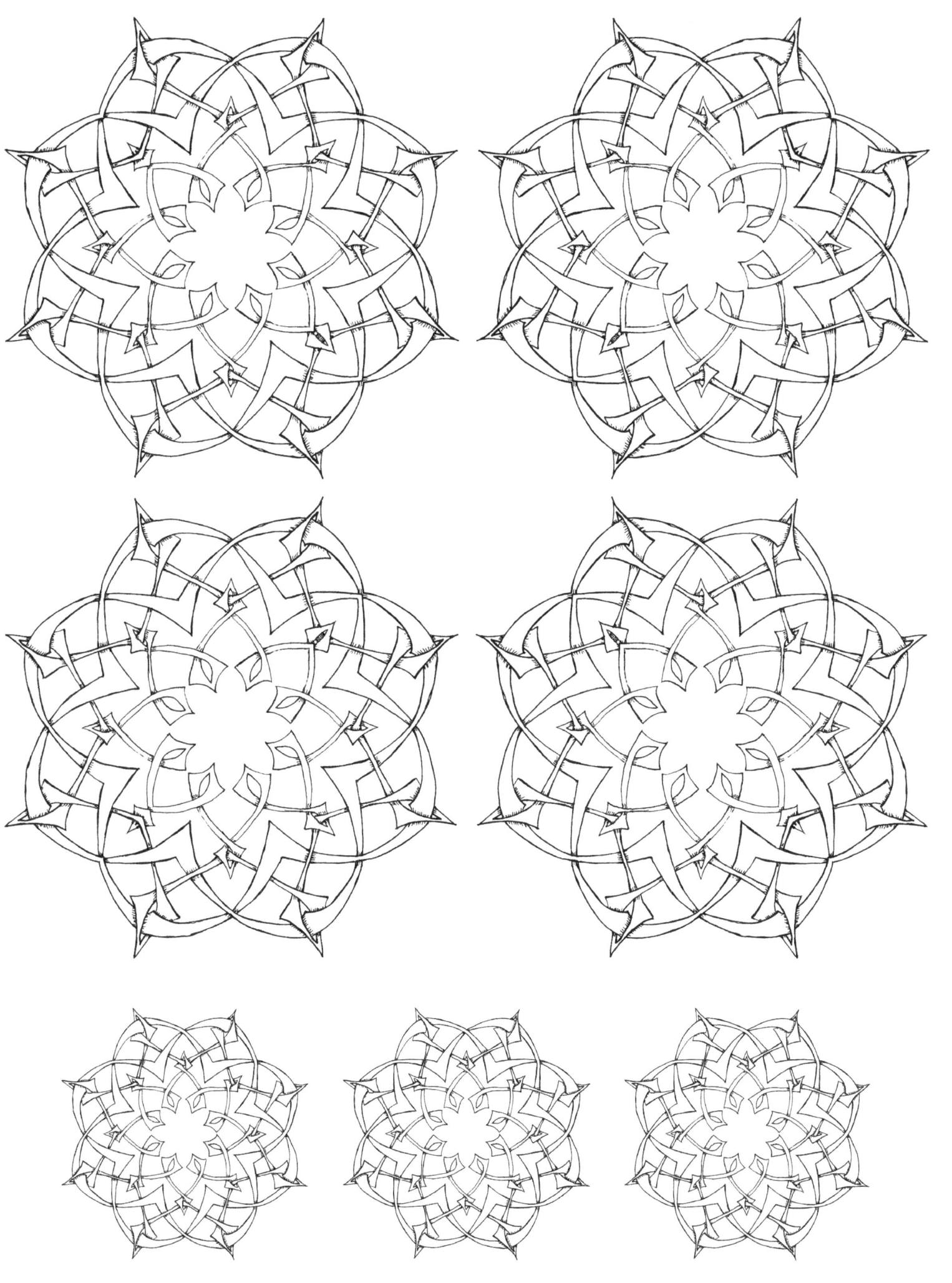

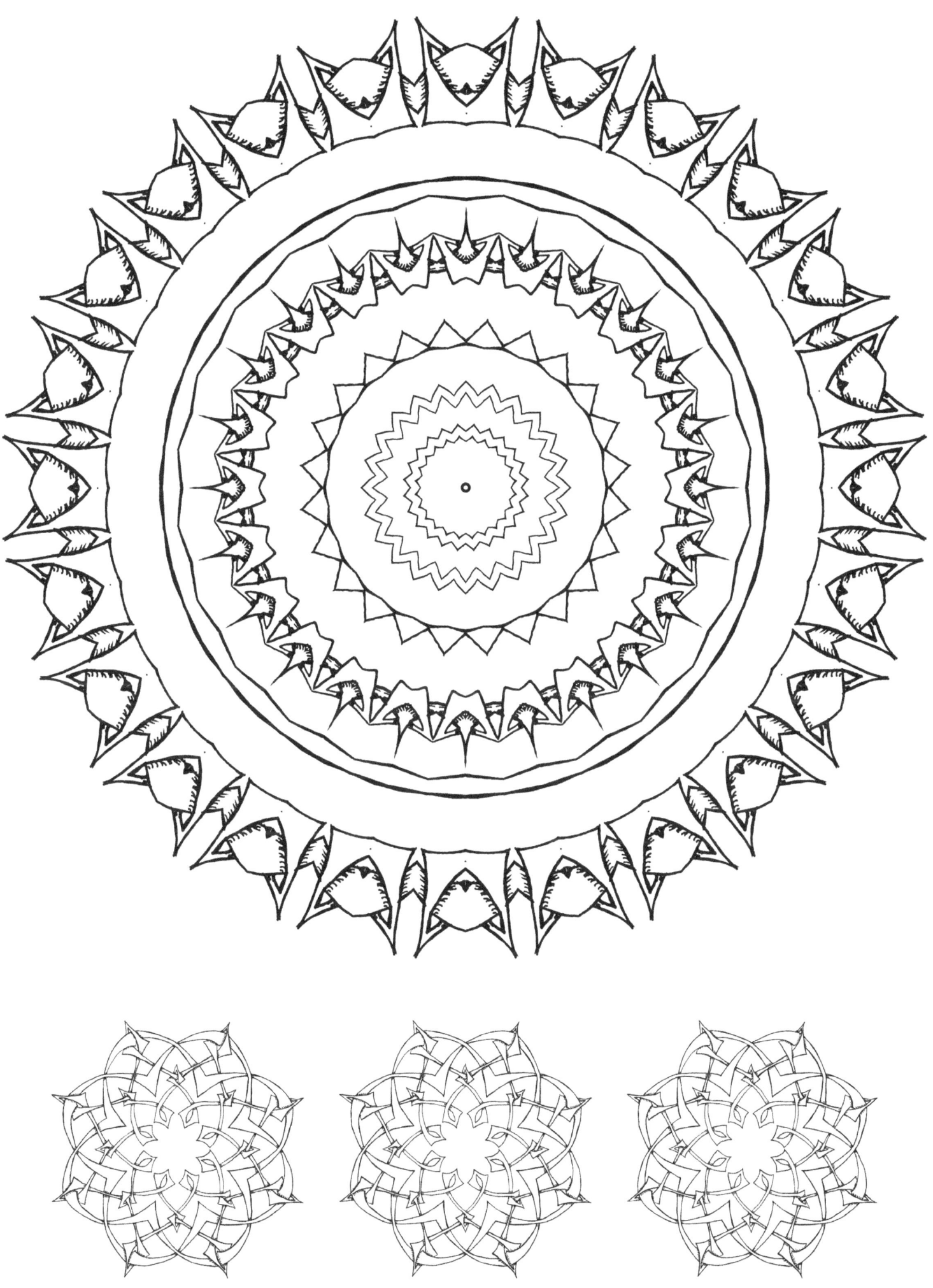

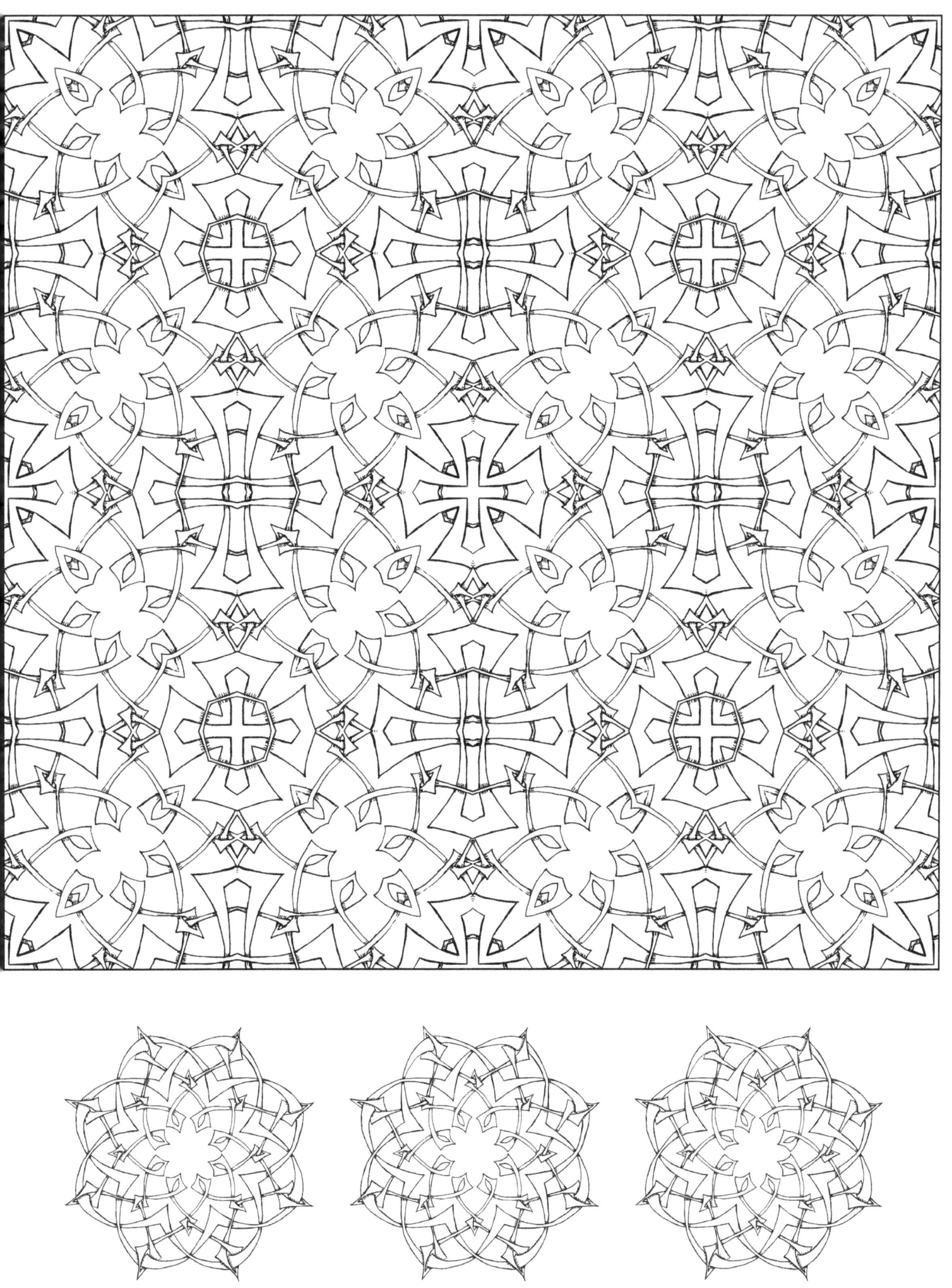

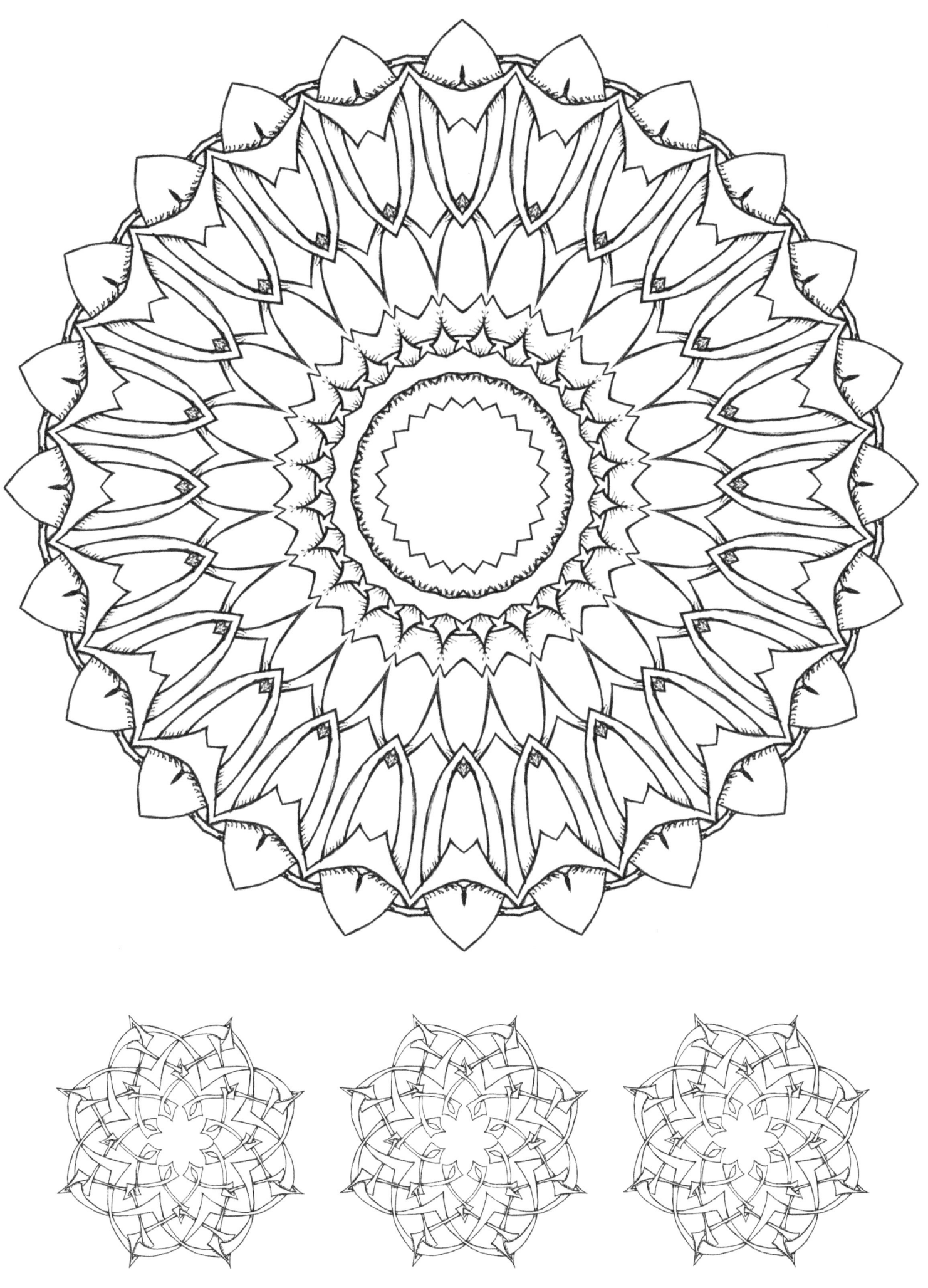

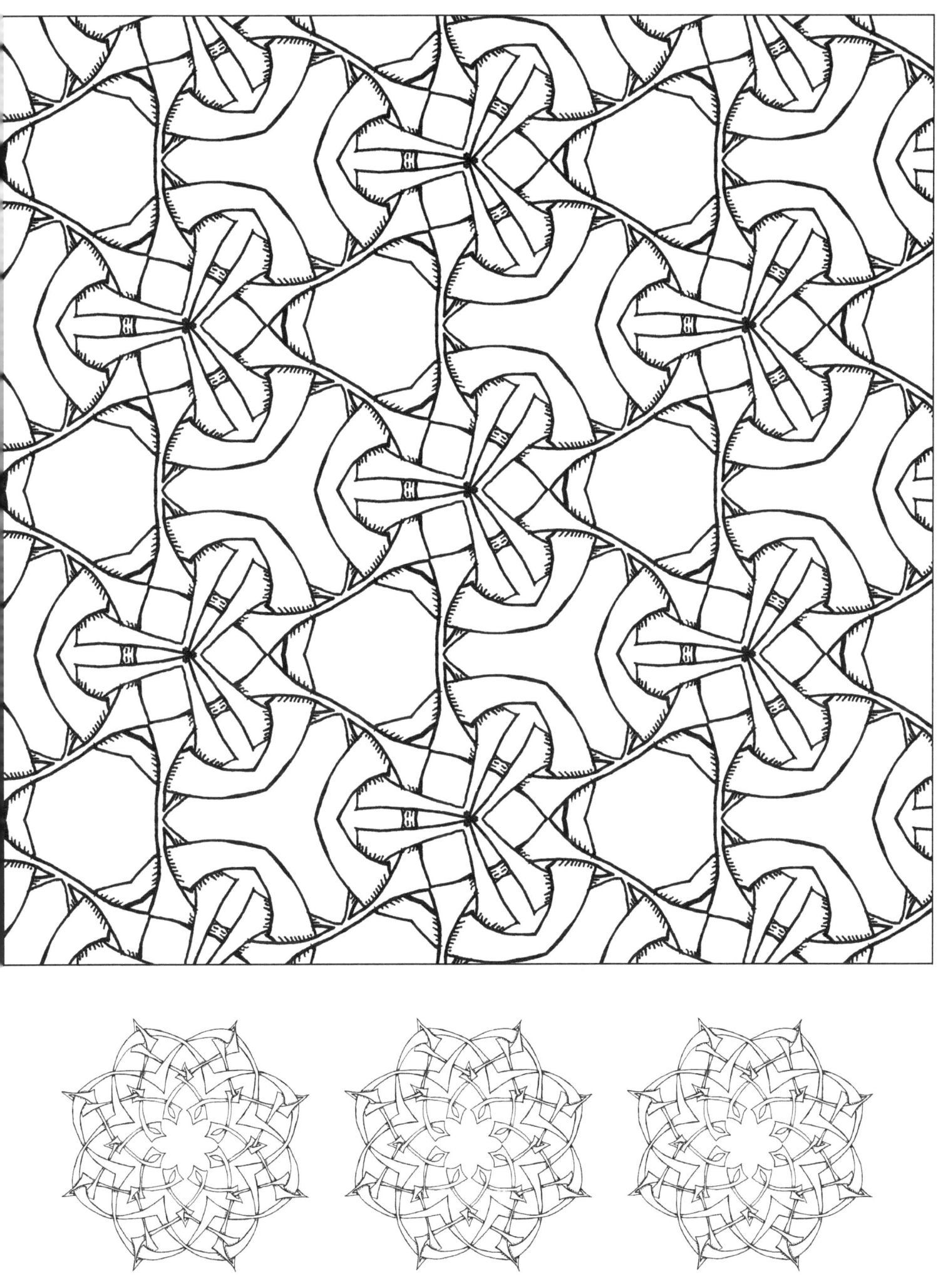

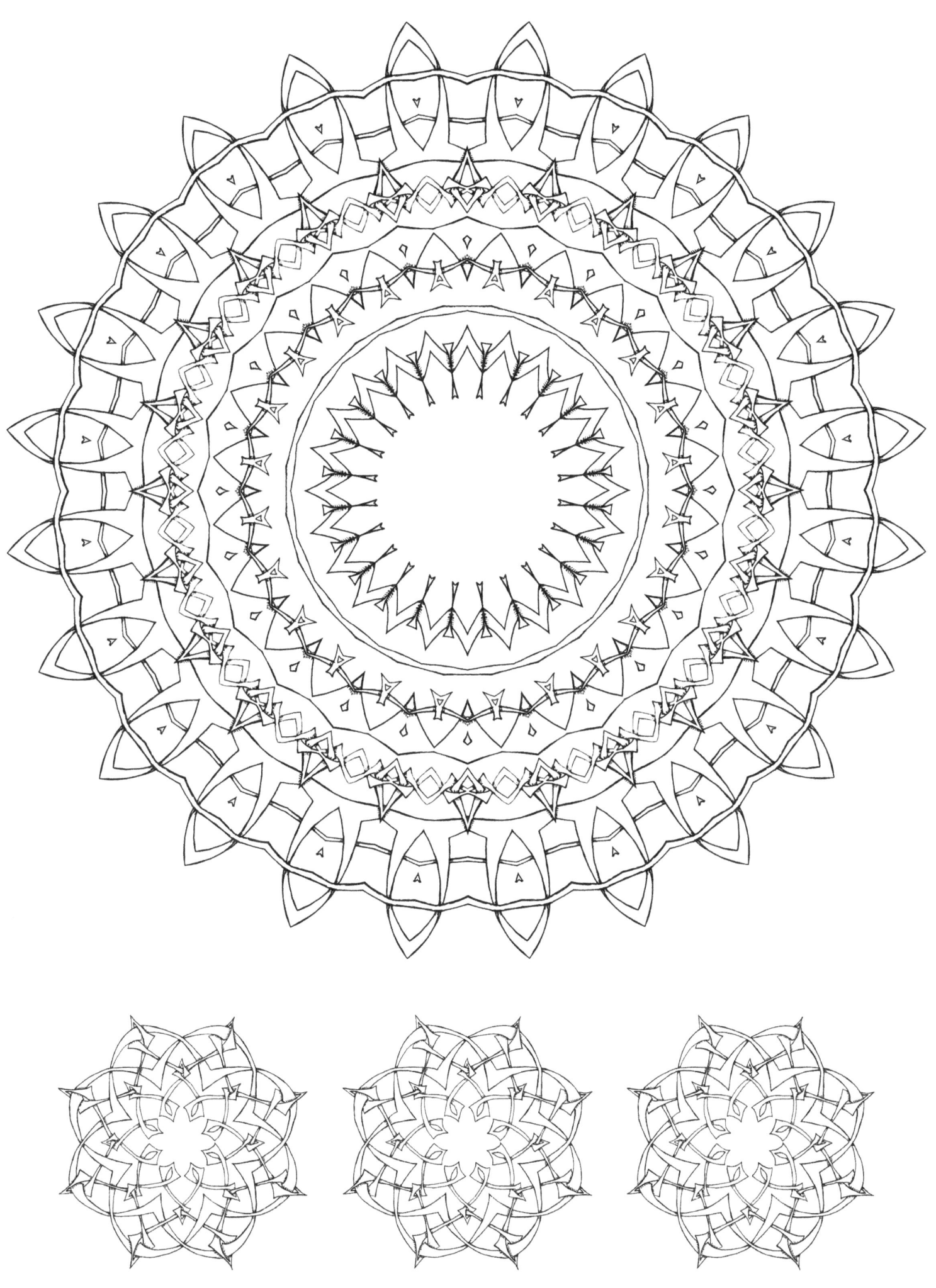

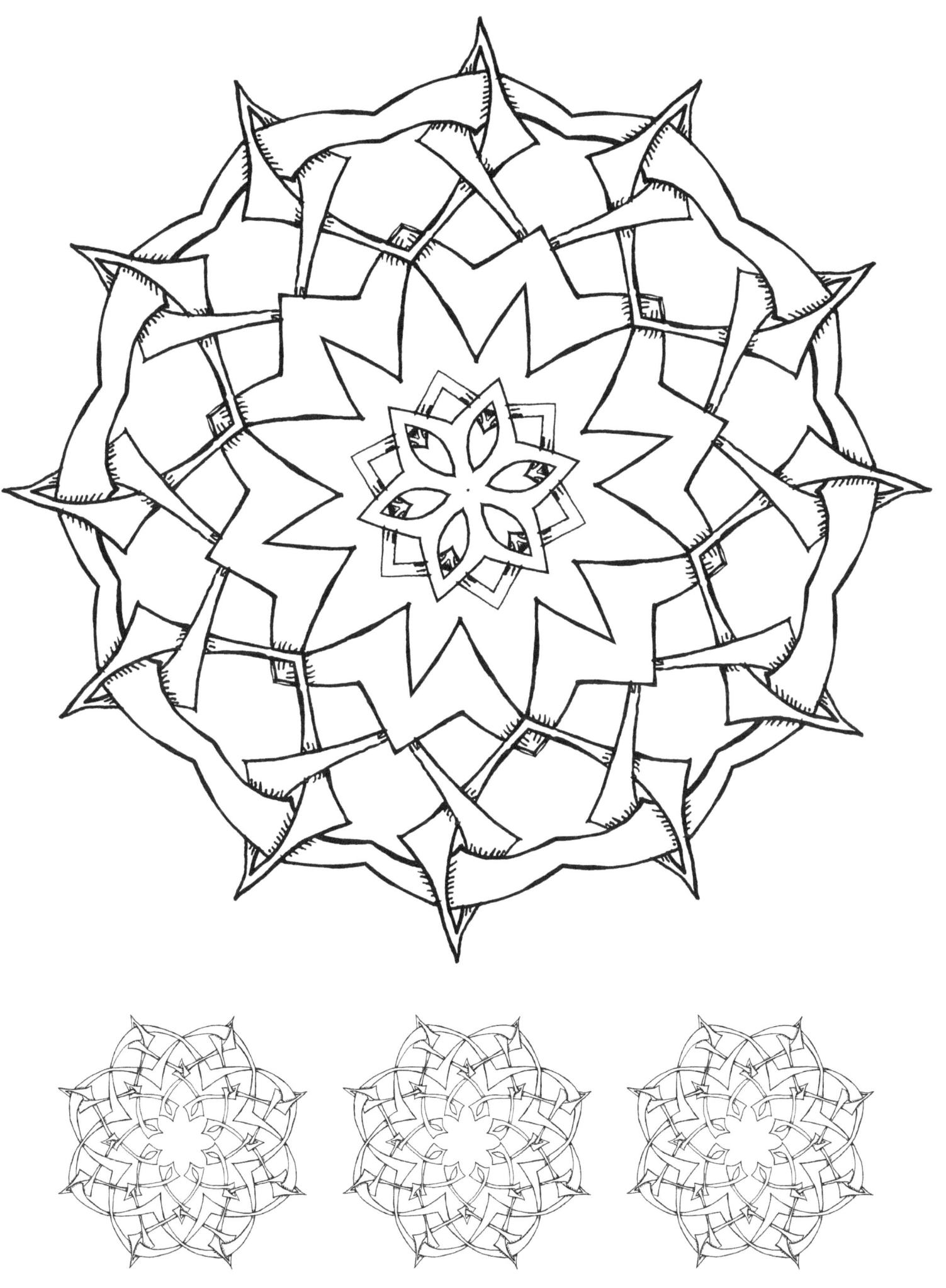

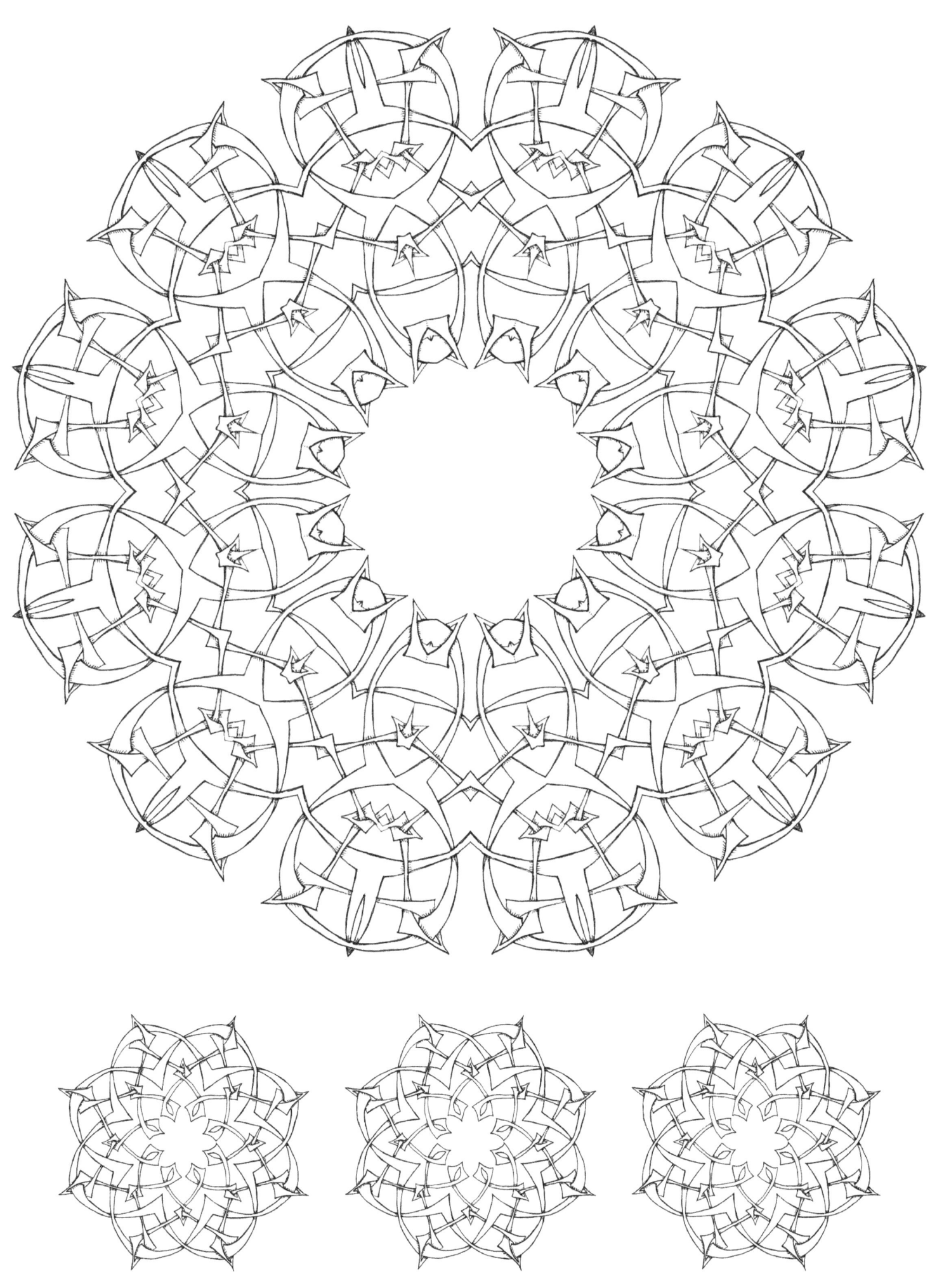

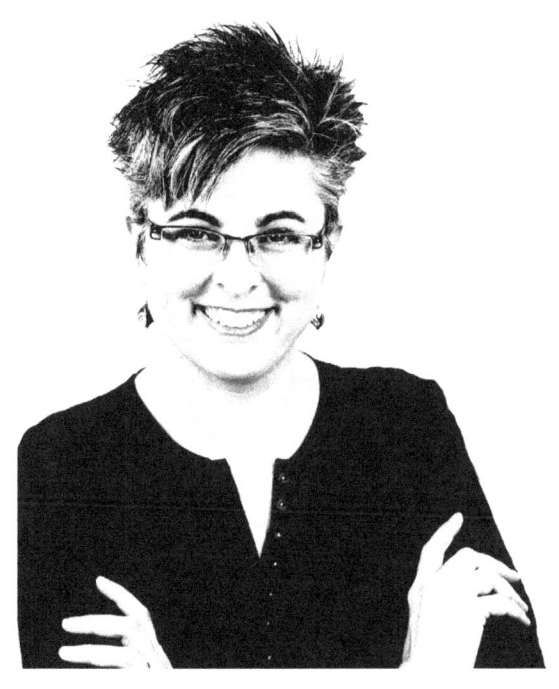

LYRIC MONTGOMERY KINARD

is an artist, author, and educator.
She transforms cloth into art in her studio
and timid spirits into confident creatives in the classroom.
You can see her work and read more about her at

www.LyricKinard.com

www.ingramcontent.com/pod-product-compliance
Lightning Source LLC
Chambersburg PA
CBHW080825170526
45158CB00009B/2526